My Body Needs Help

My Body Needs Help

Words & Pictures by Annette Abrams

Tenley Circle Press, Ltd. Washington, DC

CATALOGING IN PUBLICATION DATA
ISBN: 978-0-9773536-6-8
Library of Congress Control Number: 2011927381

Tenley Circle Press, Ltd.
P.O. Box 5625
Friendship Station
Washington, D.C. 20016
www.tenleycirclepress.com

COVER ART: Annette Abrams
BOOK DESIGN: J.A. Creative
FONT: AnnettesHand
PRINTING & BINDING: Beacon Printing Company, Inc. Waldorf, MD, USA

For All My Helper Heroes

I'm Netta. I have cancer.
I'm confused - that's really true -
I know my body needs some help -
Do you feel like that, too?

At times I'm very frightened
And often very sad –
I hate this mean old cancer –
It makes me really mad!

Sometimes I imagine
That the cancer isn't there –
Other times I feel icky
Almost everywhere.

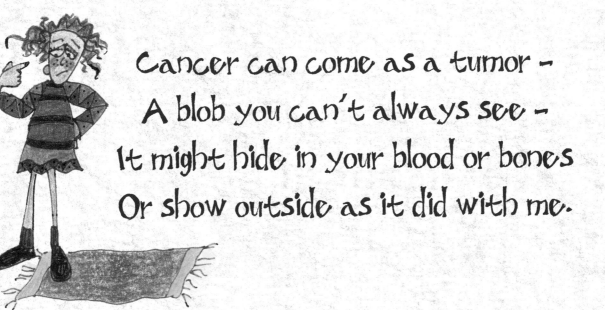

Cancer can come as a tumor –
A blob you can't always see –
It might hide in your blood or bones
Or show outside as it did with me.

Sometimes this mean old cancer
Makes my tummy hurt a lot -
At times it feels like icicles -
Other times a bubbly pot.

At times it's very hard to poop -
And my tummy feels like a big balloon
That I'm scared might suddenly pop -
I need relief real soon!

Sometimes I get headaches
That make my brain feel tight –
My eyes don't want to open –
They'd rather shut out the light.

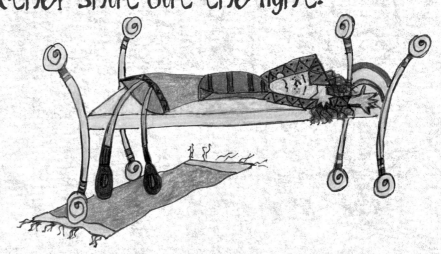

There are times I'm oh so tired
And want to sleep all day -

Other times the pain's so terrible –
Will it ever go away?

The doctors say there's a war in my body –
A battle between healthy and sick –
This cancer is the enemy –
I need help to get better – and quick!

I don't understand this cancer
Or how to make it disappear -
I cannot fight it by myself -
To me that's very clear.

I need some Helper Heroes -
Each one with a special chore -
To help my body feel its best
And make me healthy like before.

First there's my Director Doctor
In charge of the battle to win –
Leading the way for the others –
My Helper Heroes who'll all step in.

Help comes from Medication –
Pills, shots, and other meds –
And sometimes it comes from a cold pack
Or a comfy pillow for my head.

Chemo is also a Helper Hero -
It's a med with a special flair -
It's supposed to get rid of the cancer -
And it made me lose my hair.

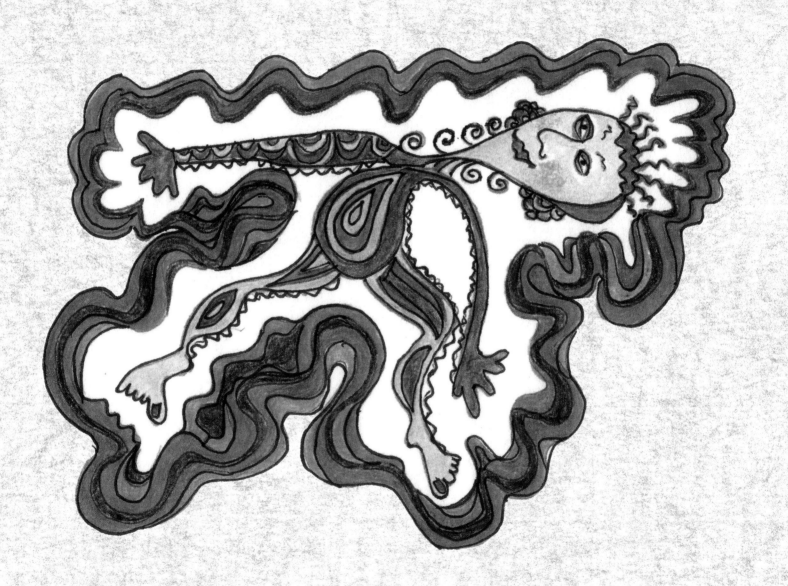

Radiation's a Helper Hero
That crushes cancer with a zap –
It can make the cancer go away
And wipe it right off the map.

Stem Cell Helper Heroes
Send cells to replace my own –
They try to destroy my cancer
And make me a cancer-free zone.

Doctors, Nurses, and Technicians
Are Guardian Angels - it's true -
They help me fight this cancer
With all the work they do.

My fabulous Family and Friends
Are Heroes who help me cope –
They try to keep my spirits up
And give me reason to hope.

My Heroes all work together -
Helping in so many ways
To win the battle inside me
And brighten up my days.

My Helper Heroes make me braver –
They help me control my fear –
They work to make me healthy –
And give me reason to cheer!

J.A. CREATIVE provides strategic marketing and creative services to businesses, non-profits, and associations. Based in Northern Virginia, J.A. Creative is owned by women who share a special interest in a healthy environment and healthy families.

BEACON PRINTING COMPANY enforces a strict recycling program and is committed to worker safety and health as an integral part of its business plan. Beacon is FSC (Forest Stewardship Council) certified and uses paper from responsibly managed forests and other controlled sources. The inks used in printing this book are vegetable based, not made from petroleum products.

Founded in 2005, TENLEY CIRCLE PRESS, LTD., is a Washington, D.C.-based publishing house producing children's books with educational, ethical, and environmentally responsible themes. Our authors, artists, editors, designers, printers, and marketing specialists share ideas and work together to produce smart, handsome books. Our books are made locally by printers who follow strong environmental, health, and safety policies. We contribute a portion of sales income every year to community-based children's health and literacy charities.

SUBSCRIBERS
as of June 30, 2011

PATRONS. Frank C. Eliot • Kashif Firozvi MD • Johns Hopkins Medicine • Lucy McBride MD
Chandler Tagliabue • Anonymous

SPONSORS. Laura Belt • Barbara Cohen • Ann Collins • Kay Dunkley • George Hnat
George Washington University Medical Center: Department of Interdisciplinary Medical Education
Peggy & Steve Hopkins • Alan & Cindy Kahan • Shirley Abrams Kahan & Family
King Hussein Cancer Foundation • Paul & Patti Knollman • Shelah Landsman
Lombardi Comprehensive Cancer Center, Georgetown University Hospital • Lyn Mueller
Nathanson Mother-Daughter Book Club • Jim Osterman • Gerald Pressman • Ingrid Rose
Lisa J. Sirota-Weiner MD • Cathy Trauernicht • Peter & Rhoda Trooboff
Susan Veras • Anonymous

FAMILY AND FRIENDS. Charlie Abrams • Joyce & Morris Abrams • Lisa Alexander
Lori Amsellem • Charlie Barker • Ellen Blackmore • Nancy Brucks • Denise Burns • Patti Chandler
Connie Cissel • Sheila Smallberg Cohen • Gail David & Steven Heydemann • Lori Dubbin
Sue Ellen Dubia • Abbie Eckland • Debbie Fink • The Giovanni-Locke Family • Ben Hayes
Catherine Hopkins • Kenny Hopkins • Sarah Hopkins • Sheila Igoe & Brian Grant • Davida Kales
Lawrence Kessner • Tammy Glatz Landy • Emmy Le Bigre • Margie Litman
Carol & Bob Luskin • Kathy Matty • Cassie Megarity • Susy Meyers • Caren Ravitch
Eleanor Rawitz • Tricia Sachs • Laurie Kaye Schwartz • The Steighner Family
Jeanne Ward • Constance Witte • Barbie & Ron Wright

Many thanks to my fabulous family, friends, and advisors, whose wise counsel and loving encouragement have made this book possible. I hope *My Body Needs Help* will help others as I have been so generously helped. -A.A.

ANNETTE ABRAMS is a wife, mother, artist, art and preschool teacher, and a recent cancer survivor who beat the odds with a stem cell transplant from her sister in 2008. During treatment at the National Institutes of Health (which she calls "an awesome place"), Annette was inspired to create many of the illustrations for *My Body Needs Help*. A graduate of the University of Maryland with a BS in Art Education, Annette is a certified early childhood educator. She lives in Bethesda, Maryland, with her "Fabulous Family of Helper Heroes."